Festivals *of the* *World*

POLAND

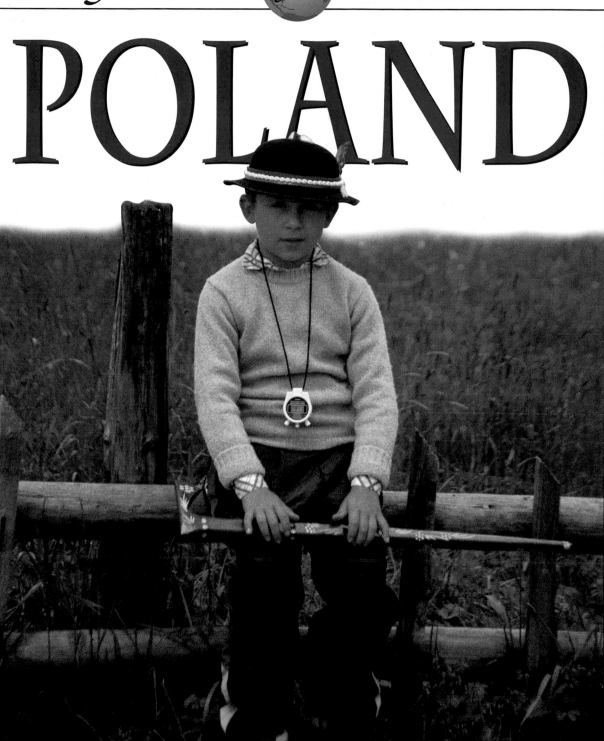

Gareth Stevens Publishing
MILWAUKEE

Written by
ALDONA MARIA ZWIERZYNSKA-COLDICOTT

Edited by
GERALDINE MESENAS

Designed by
LOO CHUAN MING

Picture research by
SUSAN JANE MANUEL

First published in North America in 1998 by
Gareth Stevens Publishing
1555 North RiverCenter Drive, Suite 201
Milwaukee, Wisconsin 53212 USA

For a free color catalog describing Gareth
Stevens' list of high-quality books and multimedia
programs, call
1-800-542-2595 (USA)
or 1-800-461-9120 (Canada).
Gareth Stevens Publishing's Fax: (414) 225-0377.
See our catalog, too, on the World Wide Web:
http://gsinc.com

© TIMES EDITIONS PTE LTD 1998
Originated and designed by
Times Books International
an imprint of Times Editions Pte Ltd
Times Centre, 1 New Industrial Road
Singapore 536196
Printed in Singapore

Library of Congress Cataloging-in-Publication Data:
Zwierzynska-Coldicott, Aldona Maria.
Poland / by Aldona Maria Zwierzynska-Coldicott.
p. cm.—(Festivals of the world)
Includes bibliographical references and index.
Summary: Describes how the culture of Poland is
reflected in its many festivals, including All Saints'
Day, Christmas, and Karnawal.
ISBN 0-8368-2018-5 (lib. bdg.)
1. Festivals—Poland—Juvenile literature. 2.
Poland—Social life and customs—Juvenile
literature. [1. Festivals—Poland. 2. Holidays—
Poland. 3. Poland—Social life and customs.]
I. Title. II. Series.
GT4871.P6Z95   1998
394.269438—dc21   98-13804

1 2 3 4 5 6 7 8 9 02 01 00 99 98

CONTENTS

It's Festival Time . . .

Festivals, called *swieta* [SVYEN-tah] in Polish, are very important to the Poles, who love celebrations and are always eager to keep tradition alive. Go on a winter sleigh ride and learn to make a Palm Sunday palm. You will see when everybody simply must have a doughnut, and you will learn to make your own delicious Easter *mazurek* [ma-ZOO-rek] cake. Would you like to meet Santa Claus and get a present on Christmas Eve? How about visiting a cemetery to pay your respects to heroes who lived a long time ago? Let's celebrate—it's another holiday in Poland!

WHERE'S POLAND?

Poland is situated in northern Europe and is one of the largest European countries. The northern part of Poland is the land of lakes, and it is mostly bordered by the Baltic Sea. Central Poland is a flat, wide-stretching plain. Along Poland's southern **frontier** are the Carpathian and the Sudeten mountains.

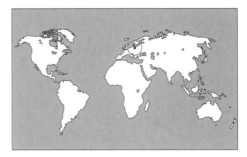

Who are the Poles?

Poland is over 1,000 years old. Throughout its history, Poland has seen many territorial conflicts and has been home to many peoples apart from the native Poles. Today, it is a stable country with few ethnic **minority groups**.

Poland has always been seen as the crossroads between Western and Eastern Europe. Much of its culture has been shaped by a mixture of influences coming from various directions.

Poles, who are a Slavic people, are friendly, hospitable, and **patriotic**. The majority of the population are Roman Catholics. Religion has always played an important role in the country. The language spoken in Poland is Polish.

A little girl in a traditional dress of red and white—the national colors of Poland. She is also wearing bead necklaces, the favorite accessories of Polish women.

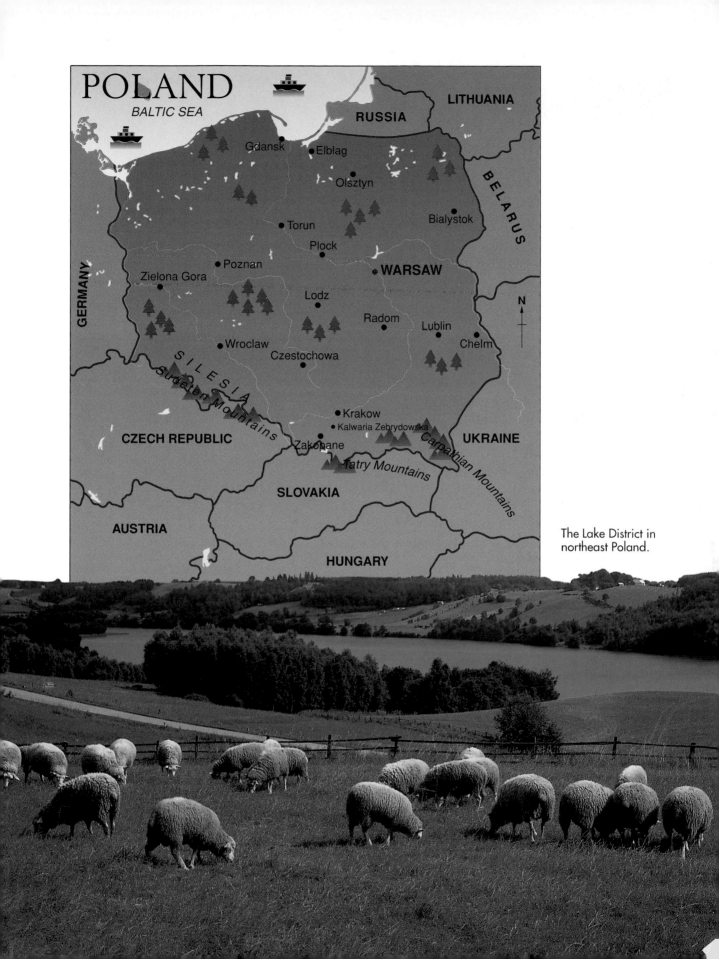

POLAND

BALTIC SEA

LITHUANIA

RUSSIA

BELARUS

GERMANY

• Gdansk
• Elblag
• Olsztyn
• Torun
• Plock
• Poznan
• Bialystok
Zielona Gora
• WARSAW
• Lodz
• Radom
• Lublin
• Wroclaw
• Chelm
Czestochowa

S I L E S I A
Sudeten Mountains

Krakow
• Kalwaria Zebrydowska
Zakopane
Tatry Mountains

CZECH REPUBLIC

UKRAINE

Carpathian Mountains

SLOVAKIA

AUSTRIA

HUNGARY

N

The Lake District in
northeast Poland.

WHEN'S THE SWIETA?

Want to see how Poles celebrate? Just flip the pages and join in the fun!

AUTUMN

- ✪ **ALL SAINTS' DAY**
- ✪ **ALL SOULS' DAY**
  - ✪ **INDEPENDENCE DAY**
  - ✪ **ST. ANDREW'S DAY**—A popular nameday (see page 7), it is traditionally the day when many dancing parties are held. For many people, it is also the best day for fortune-telling.

WINTER

- ✪ **ST. BARBARA'S DAY**—This festival is celebrated in Silesia, where coal miners parade in their black gala uniforms and tall black hats with red feathers.
- ✪ **ST. NICHOLAS'S DAY**
- ✪ **CHRISTMAS**
- ✪ **NEW YEAR'S EVE**
- ✪ **KARNAWAL**
- ✪ **EPIPHANY**—People write "K+M+B" (the initials of the three Kings) on their front doors with specially blessed chalk from church. They believe this ensures good luck in the coming year.
- ✪ **VIRGIN MARY'S DAY**—Specially decorated candles are blessed at church. People used to believe that lighting such a candle during a thunderstorm would protect the house from lightning.
- ✪ **ASH WEDNESDAY**

SPRING

- ✪ **EASTER**
- ✪ **FIRST DAY OF SPRING**—Straw dolls, called Marxanna, which **symbolize** winter, are thrown into water and "drowned" throughout the country.
- ✪ **PENTECOST**—Churches are decorated with green twigs and branches.
- ✪ **3RD MAY**—The country celebrates the anniversary of the 3rd May Constitution. Poland's constitution is the second modern one to be formed in the world, after the American Constitution.
- ✪ **CORPUS CHRISTI**

SUMMER

- ✪ **ST. JOHN'S DAY (MIDSUMMER NIGHT)**—Boys jump through bonfires on this night. Girls make special wreaths, put them on the water, and wait to see which boys will attempt to fish them out.
- ✪ **THE ASSUMPTION OF MARY**—This is one of the most important Catholic festivals in Poland. It celebrates Mary's acceptance into heaven.
- ✪ **COMMEMORATION OF WORLD WAR II**—This is celebrated on September 1st, which is also the start of the school year.
- ✪ **HARVEST FESTIVAL**—At the end of summer, Harvest Festival is celebrated throughout Poland.

I'm a participant in the St. Barbara's Day parade. To read about another festival with lots of music and fun, turn to page 16.

Namedays

Rather than birthdays, most people in Poland celebrate their given nameday, called *imieniny* [ee-mye-NEE-ny], on the appropriate day of the year—usually the feast days of the saints after whom they are named. Several names are listed in the calendar every day, and the day your name appears is your nameday. People celebrating their nameday usually receive many flowers, nameday cards, and gifts. However, they are also expected to organize a small party so relatives and friends can celebrate with them.

REMEMBERING THE DEAD

On November 1st, Poland celebrates All Saints' Day, or Wszystkich Swietych [VSHYST-keeh SVYEN-tyh], which is devoted to family members and friends who have died. On this day, Polish cemeteries overflow with people bearing flowers and wreaths to decorate the graves of loved ones. The remembrance of the dead is celebrated to a lesser degree on the following day, All Souls' Day, or Zaduszki [za-DOOSH-kee].

A little boy with a bouquet of beautiful white flowers for a loved one.

A day for memories

Imagine a November morning when cemeteries all over Poland are crowded with people. There is a steady stream of people filling all the spaces between tombstones. Everybody is busily clearing the graves of weeds and dirt, and decorating the graves with flowers, wreaths, lights, and candles. People are chatting with each other—some meeting only once a year at the graves of loved ones who have passed away.

Above: Carved wooden headstones in a cemetery in Zakopane. Poles spend large sums of money on graves and tombstones for loved ones who have died.

Right: On All Saints' Day, there are many flower stalls all around the cemeteries, crowded with people buying the prettiest flowers for their **deceased** loved ones. White flowers are the most popular.

All souls remembered

All Souls' Day is a solemn day, but not a sad one. Good times are remembered as families and friends unite to share special memories of loved ones who have died. As the day progresses, more and more people drift toward the cemeteries to light candles on the graves of family members and acquaintances—even complete strangers. After all, this is the day when no soul should be forgotten.

Left: The Tomb of the Unknown Soldier in Warsaw. It is a symbol of the thousands who died fighting for their country in World War II.

Unknown soldiers

Poland has symbolic tombs or monuments, often of unknown soldiers. These tombs were built for soldiers and other people who were killed in faraway lands during various wars—heroes who fought and died for their country. People light hundreds of candles at these monuments and pray for all these people whose final place of rest is far away from home.

Below: People pay their respects to relatives and friends who have passed away. On All Souls' Day, Polish cemeteries are filled with flowers of all colors.

May they rest in peace

Many religious processions are held around cemeteries. People write the names of deceased relatives and friends on special slips of paper, which they give to priests who will later include them in special remembrance masses.

Candles in the night

When dusk falls, the cemeteries become spectacular fields of flickering lights. You can see the yellow-red **aura** from hundreds of candles for miles around. Many people will even visit one or more cemeteries a few times to experience this special atmosphere and see the beauty of this November night.

The Katyn Tomb in Warsaw on All Souls' Day. At night, the cemeteries become beautiful visions of thousands of flickering candles.

Think about this
There are many religions that devote some days of the year to remembering the dead. Does your family set aside a day to pay respects to family and friends who have passed away? Do your friends' families do that? What other religions set aside days to remember the dead?

CHRISTMAS

ecember is Advent and Christmas time. Advent is the time of spiritual preparation for the birth of Christ. As the weeks go by, people start sending out Christmas cards, buying presents, and making plans for Christmas Eve celebrations. Churches set up nativity scenes, and some towns have competitions for the most original puppet theaters on display.

Above: Have you been naughty or nice?

Below: A colorful group singing Christmas carols.

Wigilia

For Poles, Christmas really starts on Christmas Eve when most people decorate their Christmas trees and prepare the evening feast. On this day, the first star appears in the winter sky, and families meet at elaborate Christmas Eve dinners called *Wigilia* [vee-GEE-lyah].

At the beginning of Wigilia, there may be a reading from the Bible on the story of Christ's birth in Bethlehem. After that, everyone shares the holy wafer or bread before the special Wigilia meal begins. There should not be any meat other than fish on the table, and no alcohol is allowed. There should also be 12 different courses.

One spare seat and plate are normally set for any unexpected visitor. The Polish believe nobody should be turned away from the door on Christmas Eve.

A typical example of a Christmas Eve dinner—called the Wigilia—in Poland.

For the children only

The Wigilia dinner is also the time when presents appear under the Christmas tree. When the feast is finished, children are usually itching to unwrap the presents and find out if they have received what they had wished for in their letters to St. Nicholas or Santa Claus. Sometimes, the good Saint appears in person with his sack of goodies and asks all the usual questions to **determine** if the child has been good or naughty. After that, he distributes the goodies before he quietly disappears again to continue his sleigh journey to other houses and other excited children.

Above: The midnight mass, called the Pasterka, on Christmas Eve. Notice the nativity scene on the right of the altar.

St. Nicholas

In fact, the **anticipation** of presents starts much earlier than Christmas Eve for children. December 6th is St. Nicholas's Day. This is every Polish child's favorite day. On this day, St. Nicholas, called *Swiety Mikolaj* [SVYEN-tyh mee-KOH-way], comes at night and leaves small presents in children's shoes. However, children who have been naughty may find a small bunch of silver or golden painted twigs instead. These are warnings to these naughty children to start mending their ways or St. Nicholas will not give them a gift or reward at Christmas.

Left: A Christmas puppet theater in Krakow.

Pasterka

After all the excitement of Wigilia, the family usually relaxes by chatting, singing carols, or watching television. At midnight, everyone prepares to go to church for a special midnight mass called *Pasterka* [pah-STERR-kah]. You can also watch it televised from Rome, where it is celebrated by the Pope—who is a Pole himself! Christmas Day and Boxing Day, which are also traditionally called the First and the Second Day of the Holidays, are usually spent with family and close friends. Christmas is the time to rest and enjoy the season. The Christmas season is also a popular time for weddings.

Think about this

According to an old tradition, a small, sweet-smelling spruce tree is hung from the rafters on Christmas Eve. If a young man notices a young woman under the dangling spruce tree, he is allowed to kiss her. Do you know of another plant that Americans hang at Christmas time that has the same qualities as the Polish spruce tree?

These men are competing for a prize for the most beautiful Christmas puppet theater. The most famous competition takes place in Krakow every year.

KARNAWAL

After the four weeks of Advent, there is a lot of rejoicing when Christmas finally arrives. However, most people in Poland become really festive after Christmas, during the carnival period called Karnawal [karr-NAH-vow]. Karnawal lasts for the first few weeks of the year and ends on Shrove Tuesday.

Sylwester

There are many private parties and formal balls during Karnawal, which starts with the lively celebrations of New Year's Eve—known as *Sylwester* [syl-VE-sterr] in Poland, after a man's nameday on December 31st. Polish people enjoy partying and meeting their friends, so small private parties are extremely popular. Dancing is one of Poland's favorite national activities. Everybody welcomes an occasion to practice their dancing skills on the floor. Both the older and the younger generations enjoy dancing in pairs.

Above and *left:* Young people celebrate the night away at the Sylwester Ball outside the Royal Palace in Warsaw.

Costume parties

However, the fun of Karnawal is not only for adults.
Children attend their own special parties, called *choinka*
[ho-IN-kah], meaning "the Christmas Tree party," since the
tree plays an important role in the party. These are often
costume parties where little princes and princesses, fairies,
and snowflakes **mingle** with batmen, cowboys, and ninjas.
There are always many competitions, games, and dances.
Often, a popular film or a cartoon will be shown. Most
important of all, there is usually a visit from Santa Claus
carrying a sack full of fruit, candies, and all sorts of gifts.

Kulig

In the countryside, there is an old tradition of the carnival *kulig* [KOO-lik], or sleigh rides, which used to be popular among the Polish **gentry**. In the past, several people would ride through the snow-covered forest in the evening. The women would ride in sleighs, and the men would be on horseback. The participants would pay an unexpected visit to a neighbor who would then have to entertain them with food and music. After that, the neighbor would ride with the kulig to the next manor house, where they would have more feasting and dancing before setting out for other houses in the vicinity. Sometimes, the kulig would go around for the whole night until its participants were completely exhausted. Today, the kulig usually lasts a few hours and consists of a sleigh ride with torches to the forest. It usually ends with a big bonfire, over which the participants fry sausages and keep themselves warm. There may also be some singing, dancing, and drinking before everyone heads back to the village.

The Highlanders' Carnival in the Tatry Mountains.

Left: A children's costume party in a school in Warsaw.

Think about this

Do you know of another festival where people **disguise** themselves as superheroes, witches, goblins, princesses, and other crazy costumes and disguises?

Fat Thursday

Karnawal ends when the 40-day period of Lent begins. The last Thursday before Lent is called Fat Thursday, when people in Poland eat jam doughnuts as a symbol of a good and plentiful Karnawal. Shrove Tuesday is the last day of Karnawal, with many farewell parties before the season of fasting.

Below: The carnival kulig is still celebrated today, when family and friends gather for music, food, and laughter.

HOLY WEEK

In the past, people observed Lent fasting in a very strict fashion, but today, they mainly avoid eating meat on Fridays and have only two meals on Good Friday. The last week of Lent is known as Holy Week and is always a busy time for Polish women as they prepare for Easter, which falls on the last day of the week. Easter preparations include house cleaning and baking traditional *mazurek* and *baba* [BAH-bah] cakes.

Above: A Palm Sunday procession. In Poland, competitions are held for the best Easter palms—some are as tall as 33 feet (10 meters)!

Palm Sunday

On Palm Sunday, the whole family goes to church with colorful palms of all sizes. In some regions, they are just willow twigs with white catkins. However, in many towns and villages, the palms are made of grasses and dried flowers and are real objects of art. In some regions, the Easter palms can sometimes be as tall as 33 feet (10 meters)!

Left: Two girls in traditional costumes, carrying tall palms on Palm Sunday.

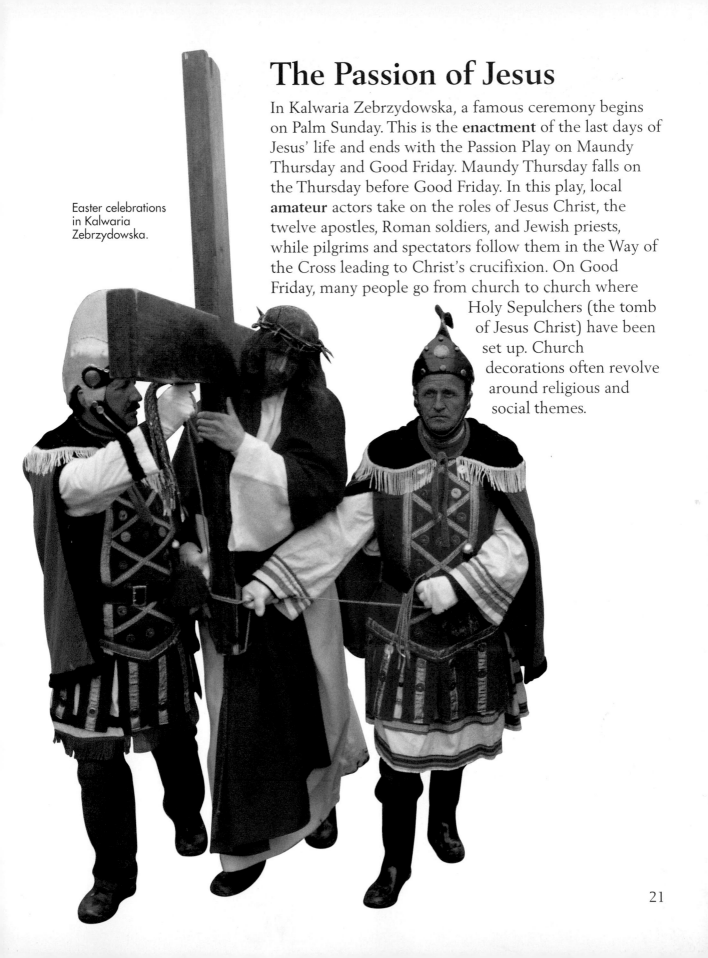

The Passion of Jesus

In Kalwaria Zebrzydowska, a famous ceremony begins on Palm Sunday. This is the **enactment** of the last days of Jesus' life and ends with the Passion Play on Maundy Thursday and Good Friday. Maundy Thursday falls on the Thursday before Good Friday. In this play, local **amateur** actors take on the roles of Jesus Christ, the twelve apostles, Roman soldiers, and Jewish priests, while pilgrims and spectators follow them in the Way of the Cross leading to Christ's crucifixion. On Good Friday, many people go from church to church where Holy Sepulchers (the tomb of Jesus Christ) have been set up. Church decorations often revolve around religious and social themes.

Easter celebrations in Kalwaria Zebrzydowska.

Holy Saturday and Easter

On Holy Saturday, all the churches fill with adults and children carrying decorated baskets containing eggs, bread, sausages, cakes, salt, and pepper to be blessed by the priest. On Easter Sunday morning, all the blessed food is eaten during the ceremonial breakfast when all the members of the family wish one another well.

Easter is a family holiday. All public life stops for two days, and people relax and feast. Symbols of Easter in Poland include colorfully painted eggs, palms, sugar lambs, ducklings, chickens, and bunnies.

Opposite: A priest blesses and sprinkles holy water over Easter baskets on Holy Saturday.

Below: Easter Monday is a holiday and is widely known as a lucky day for weddings and other ceremonies. This day is also called Wet Monday because people traditionally sprinkle each other with water on this day. A person may be splattered with just a few drops or drenched with a whole bucketful of water!

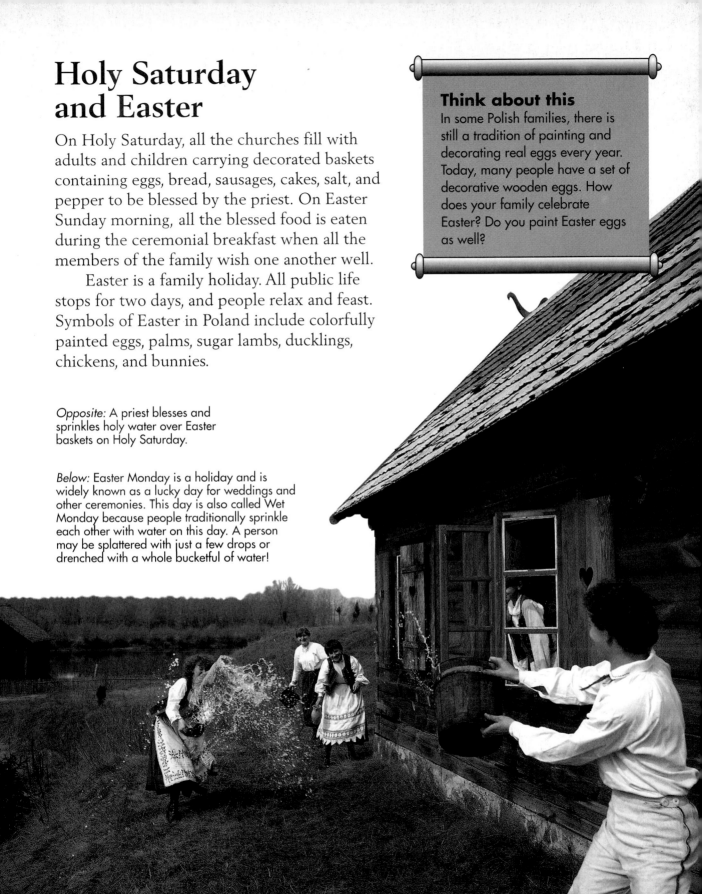

CORPUS CHRISTI

Below: Little girls wear white First Communion dresses in the Corpus Christi procession.

Corpus Christi, or the Feast of the Body of Christ, is an official holiday celebrated on the first Thursday after Whit Sunday, which falls on the seventh Sunday after Easter. This festival celebrates the presence of Christ in the sacrament of the Eucharist.

Four altars are constructed in the streets of the town or the fields in the country. These become the four stops of a special procession, which usually starts in the morning from the main local church, proceeding from one altar to the next and ending at the church where it started.

Above: Young boys join the Corpus Christi procession.

The procession

The procession is centered around the monstrance, a beautifully decorated container for the holy bread, which is carried by a priest. Little girls in white First Communion dresses walk before the priests, carrying baskets of colorful flower petals, which they throw on the ground to decorate the way for the monstrance. Other procession participants follow close behind, carrying religious pictures. There are usually many priests and church officials, who lead the prayers among the crowd.

The procession also includes disabled people and representatives from the various professions. At each altar, the monstrance is displayed, and the people kneel on the street as they pray and listen to readings from the Bible. Corpus Christi is a special day for the Polish church.

Above: A marching band in the Corpus Christi procession.

Below: Priests carry the monstrance, which contains the holy bread.

THINGS FOR YOU TO DO

The Polish are a very patriotic people, and Poland was the first country in Central and Eastern Europe to end communist rule. At the same time, Poland has a rich culture in arts and handicrafts. The Polish are also very skilled craftspeople.

Make a Polish flag

The Polish flag is the pride of the nation. To make a paper flag, you need a stick, two rectangular pieces of paper—a white one and a red one—and glue. First, glue the two pieces of paper together lengthwise. Make sure the white piece is slightly on top of the red piece. Put some glue on the shorter end of the red and white flag, and wrap it around the stick. When you're done, you will have a symbol of the Poles' patriotism in your hands!

Make a paper lace serviette

This is a very popular craft in various parts of Poland. Take a square sheet of paper. Fold it horizontally in two, and then fold it again vertically. You can also fold the paper diagonally. Then, start cutting a pattern at the corners and along the edges of the folded paper. Take care not to cut off an entire folded edge. With a smaller pair of scissors, cut the inside of the folded paper for more beautiful patterns. When you have finished, unfold the whole sheet of paper. You should see a symmetrical pattern of holes and cuts, forming a paper lace serviette or picture. Show your paper lace serviette off to your friends and hold lace serviette contests to see whose is the most beautiful!

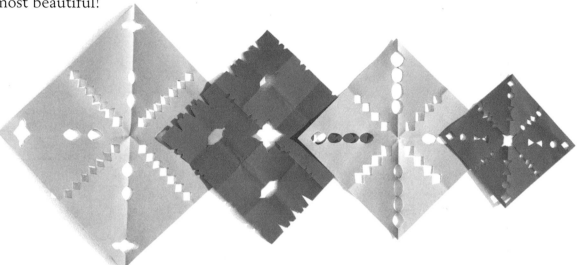

Things to look for in your library

The Angel's Mistake: Stories of Chelm. Francine Prose (Greenwillow, 1997).

Child of the Warsaw Ghetto. David A. Adler (Holiday House, 1995).

Jacob's Rescue: A Holocaust Story. Malka Drucker and Michael Halperin (Bantam Skylark, 1993).

Marie Curie. Ibi Lepscky, Marcel Danesi (translator) (Barrons Juveniles, 1993).

Poland (Remastered). Tangerine Dream (compact disk, 1996).

Poland (Postcards from). Denise Allard (Raintree/Steck Vaughn, 1996).

Poland: Land of Freedom Fighters (Discovering our Heritage). Christine Pfeiffer (Dillon Pr, 1991).

Polish Christmas Traditions. (http://www.polamjournal.com/library/christmas.html, 1997).

The Trumpeter of Krakow. Eric Philbrook Kelly (Aladdin Paperbacks, 1992).

MAKE A PALM SUNDAY PALM

O n Palm Sunday, Easter palms are made all over Poland. Some regions hold palm competitions, where the most beautiful palm wins. In these contests, the palms can be as tall as 33 feet (10 meters)! You can make your very own Palm Sunday palm, too! Be creative and use your favorite flowers.

You will need:
1. Tall decorative grasses
2. Glue
3. Scissors
4. String
5. Decorative coil or printed ribbon
6. Tape
7. Small, dried flowers of different colors

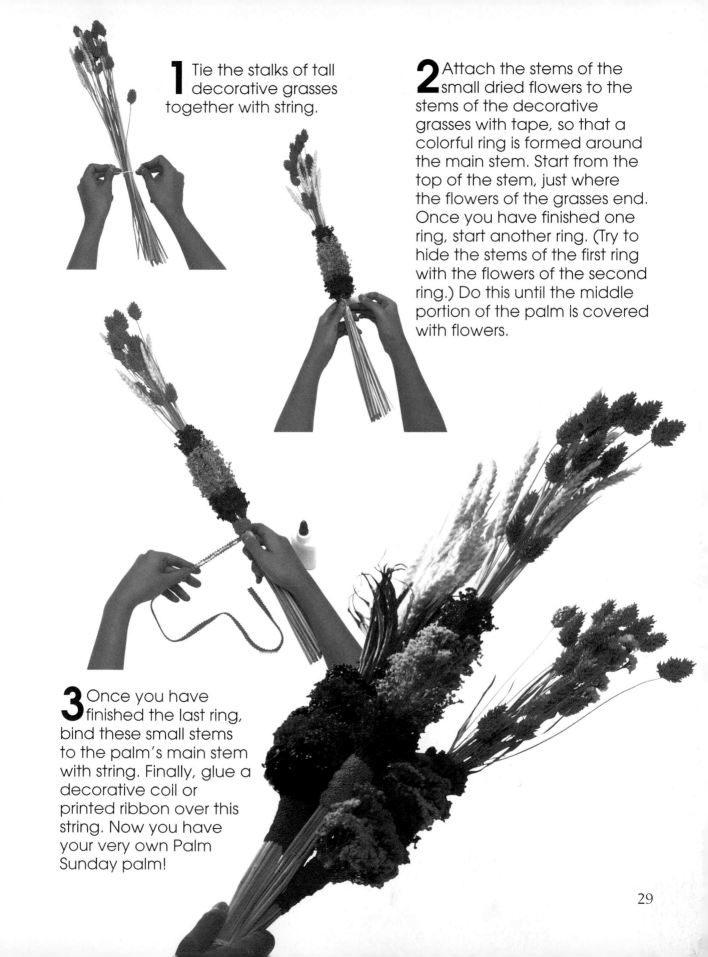

1 Tie the stalks of tall decorative grasses together with string.

2 Attach the stems of the small dried flowers to the stems of the decorative grasses with tape, so that a colorful ring is formed around the main stem. Start from the top of the stem, just where the flowers of the grasses end. Once you have finished one ring, start another ring. (Try to hide the stems of the first ring with the flowers of the second ring.) Do this until the middle portion of the palm is covered with flowers.

3 Once you have finished the last ring, bind these small stems to the palm's main stem with string. Finally, glue a decorative coil or printed ribbon over this string. Now you have your very own Palm Sunday palm!

MAKE NUT MAZUREK

The traditional Nut Mazurek cake is the highlight of Easter, where there is lots of feasting and celebrations to celebrate the resurrection of Christ. Get an adult to help you use the oven when you bake this delicious Polish treat.

You will need:
1. ½ cup (60 g) whole almonds
2. Chocolate frosting
3. 5 egg whites
4. ¾ cup (90 g) powdered sugar
5. ½ cup (100 g) ground almonds
6. 1 teaspoon of flour
7. Large mixing bowl
8. Baking tray
9. Pot holder
10. Butter knife
11. Chopping board
12. Whisk
13. Measuring spoons
14. 2 teaspoons of butter

1 Use a whisk to whip the egg whites and the powdered sugar together until they become like a stiff cream.

2 Mix in the ground almonds.

3 Cover the baking tray with a thin layer of butter and sprinkle it with flour. Pour the mixture into the baking tray. Bake at 350°F (175°C) for 35 to 40 minutes.

4 When the mazurek base is done, let it cool down. Then, spread a layer of chocolate icing over the top of the cake with a butter knife and decorate it with halved almonds. Your delicious nut mazurek cake is ready to be served!

GLOSSARY

amateur, 21	A person inexperienced or unskilled in a particular activity.
anticipation, 14	Expectation or hope.
aura, 11	Light or radiance.
deceased, 9	No longer living; dead.
determine, 14	To conclude or ascertain after observation.
disguise, 19	To change your appearance so as to hide your identity, as with costumes, masks, etc.
enactment, 21	The process of representing in a play.
frontier, 4	The part of the country that borders another country.
gentry, 18	Wellborn and well-bred people.
mingle, 17	To mix in company.
minority groups, 4	Groups differing from the majority of a population, in race, religion, ethnic background, etc.
patriotic, 4	Characteristic of people who love and support their country.
symbolize, 7	To stand for or represent something.

INDEX